Ea

MW00700680

Halloween At Its Best!

Book 1

Contents

Look at the Witches

Elizabeth W. Greenleaf

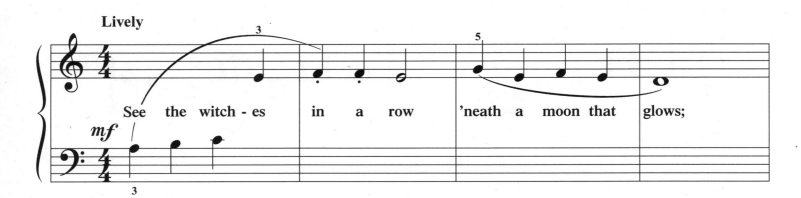

See the witch - es in a row 'neath a moon that glows;

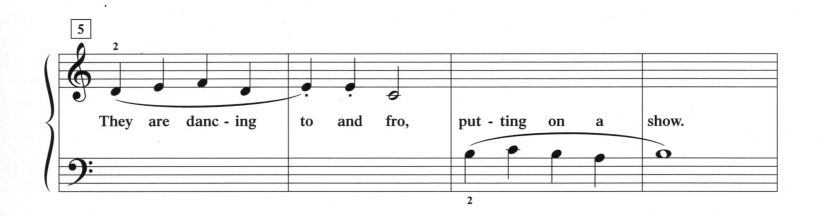

They are danc - ing to and fro, put - ting on a show.

Teacher Duet: (Student plays 1 octave higher)

Copyright © 2001 The FJH Music Company Inc. (ASCAP).
International Copyright Secured.   Made in U.S.A.   All Rights Reserved.

FJH2153

Wib - ble wob - ble go their hats; "me - ow" go their cats.

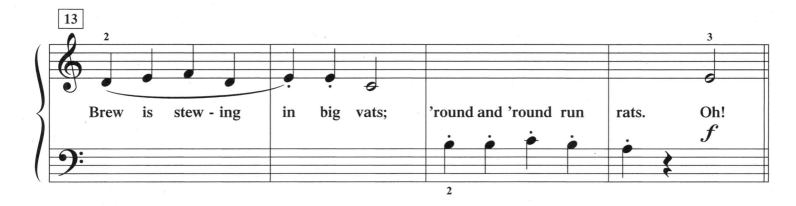

Brew is stew - ing in big vats; 'round and 'round run rats. Oh!

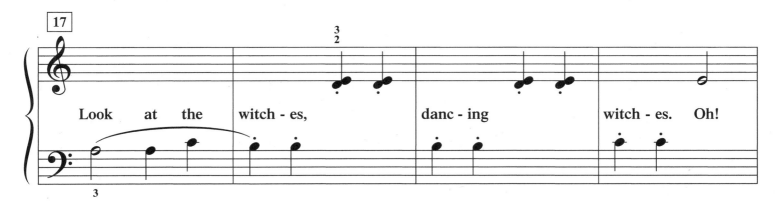

Look at the witch - es, danc - ing witch - es. Oh!

Look at the witch - es. See their fan - cy

mp

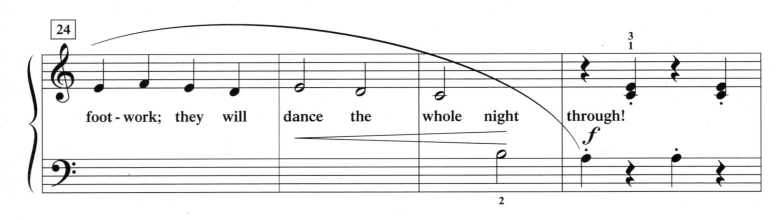

foot - work; they will dance the whole night through!

f

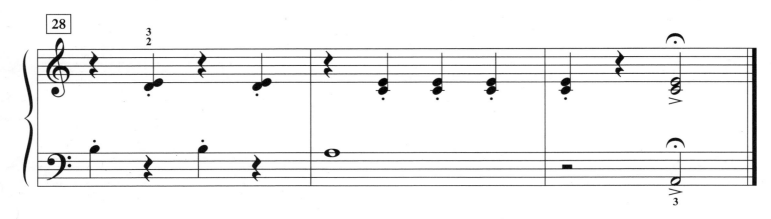

Halloween Boo!

Melody Bober

Carefully! (♩ = 160)

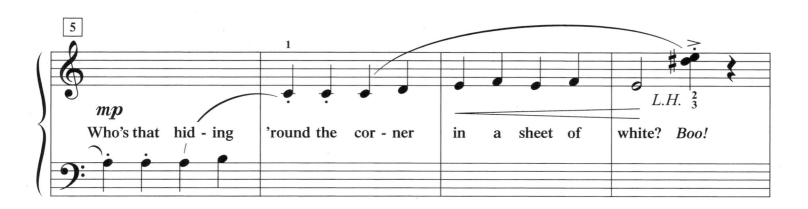

Who's that hid - ing 'round the cor - ner in a sheet of white? *Boo!*

Teacher Duet: (Student plays 1 octave higher)

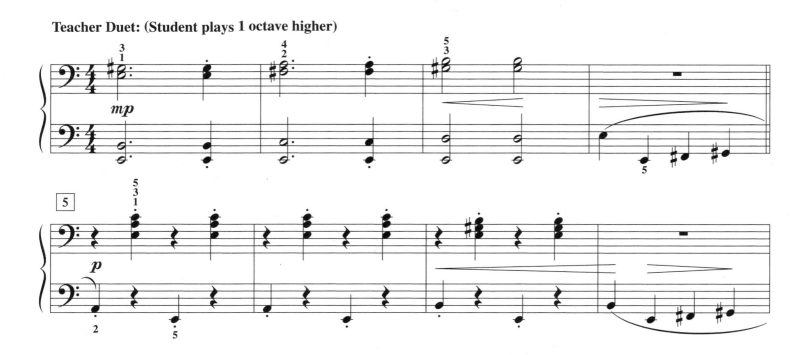

Copyright © 2004 The FJH Music Company Inc. (ASCAP).
International Copyright Secured.   Made in U.S.A.   All Rights Reserved.

FJH2153

Some-one wants to fright-en me on Hal-low-een night!

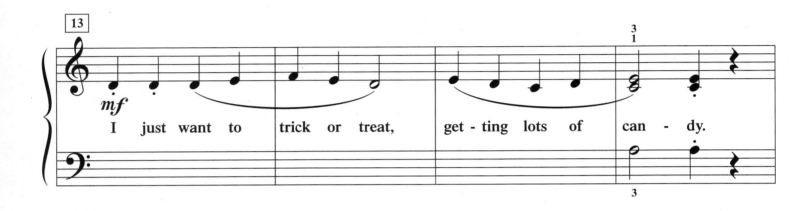

I just want to trick or treat, get-ting lots of can - dy.

I don't like the scar-y stuff! I think may-be I will

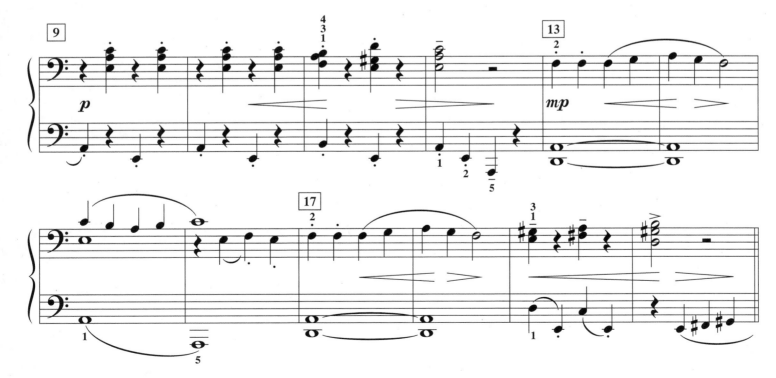

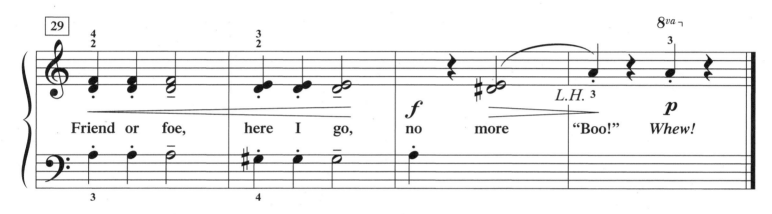

A Spooky Halloween

Elizabeth W. Greenleaf

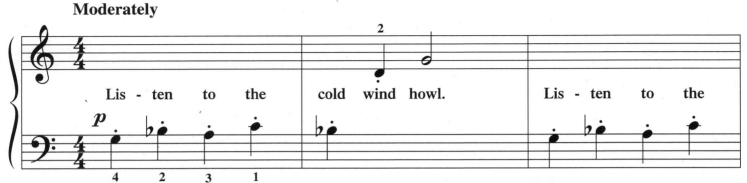

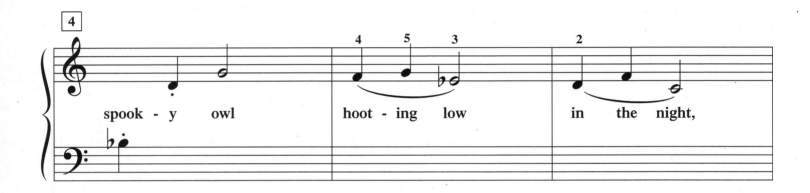

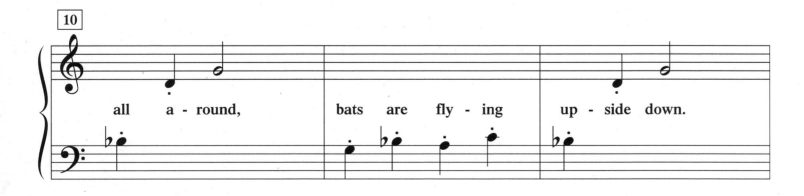

Copyright © 1997 The FJH Music Company Inc. (ASCAP).
International Copyright Secured.   Made in U.S.A.   All Rights Reserved.

13

Ghosts are seen. Hal - lo - ween! It's a spook - y

16

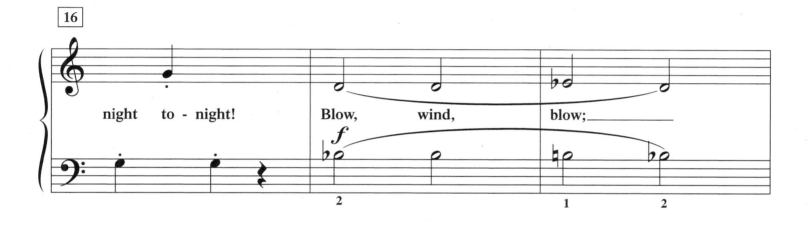

night to - night! Blow, wind, blow;

19

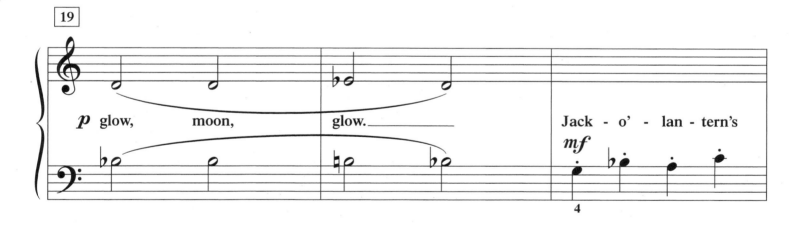

glow, moon, glow. Jack - o' - lan - tern's

22

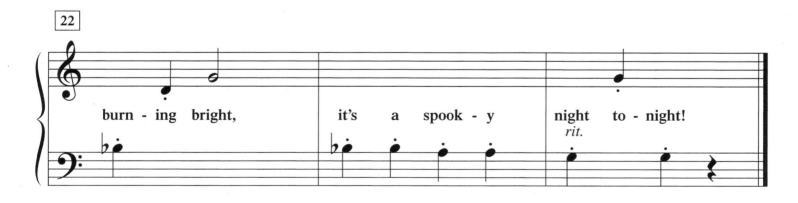

burn - ing bright, it's a spook - y night to - night!

rit.

for Justin Kuhn

A Frightful Night

Mary Leaf

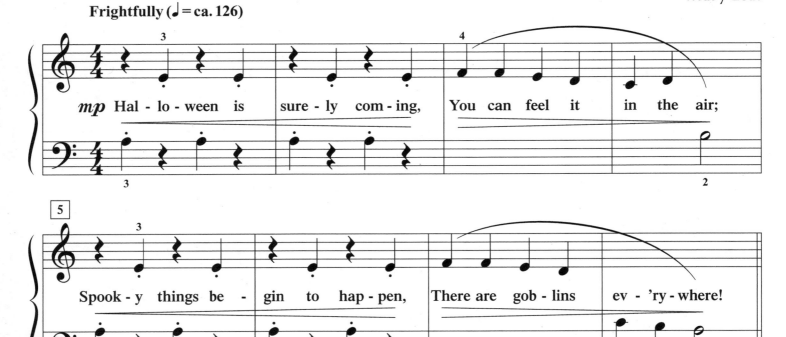

Halloween is surely coming, You can feel it in the air;

Spooky things begin to happen, There are goblins ev'rywhere!

Teacher Duet: (Student plays as written)

Copyright © 2002 The FJH Music Company Inc. (ASCAP).
International Copyright Secured.   Made in U.S.A.   All Rights Reserved.

The Piano-Playing Skeleton

Kevin and Julia Olson

Teacher Duet: (Student plays 1 octave higher)

Copyright © 2007 The FJH Music Company Inc. (ASCAP).
International Copyright Secured.   Made in U.S.A.   All Rights Reserved.

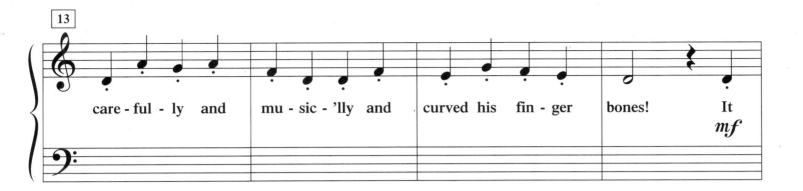

care - ful - ly and | mu - sic - 'lly and | curved his fin - ger | bones! It *mf*

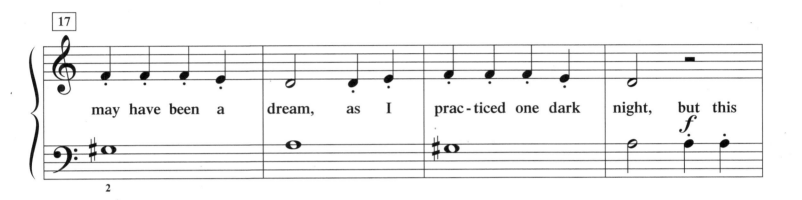

may have been a | dream, as I | prac - ticed one dark | night, but this *f*

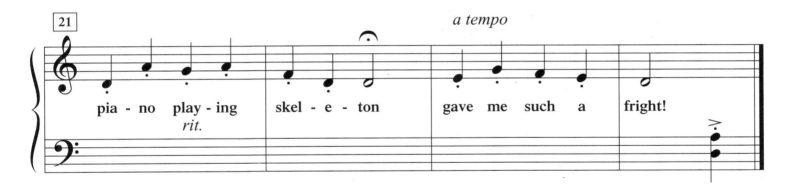

a tempo

pia - no play - ing *rit.* | skel - e - ton | gave me such a | fright!

The Worst Ghost

Elizabeth W. Greenleaf

Spookily

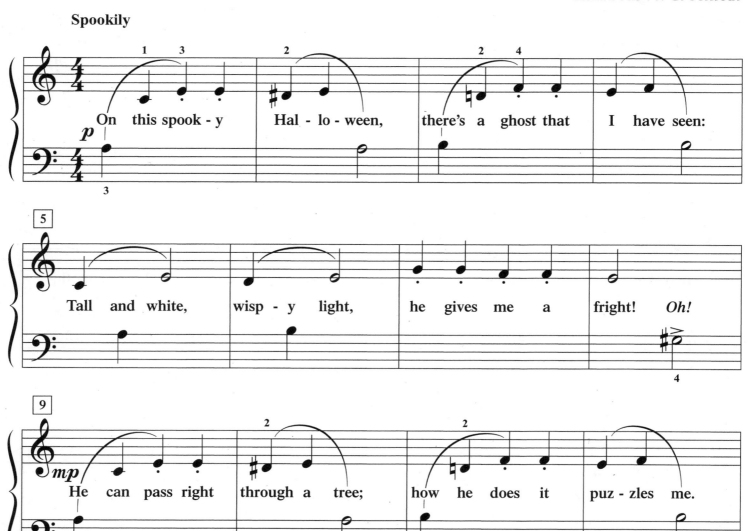

Teacher Duet: (Student plays 1 octave higher, without pedal)

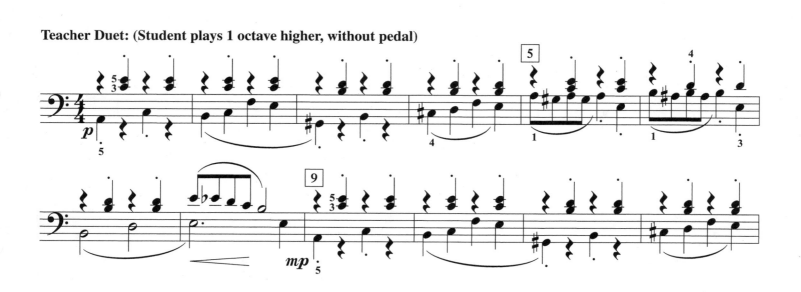

Copyright © 2003 The FJH Music Company Inc. (ASCAP).
International Copyright Secured.   Made in U.S.A.   All Rights Reserved.

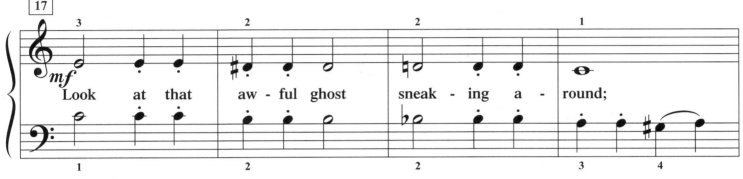

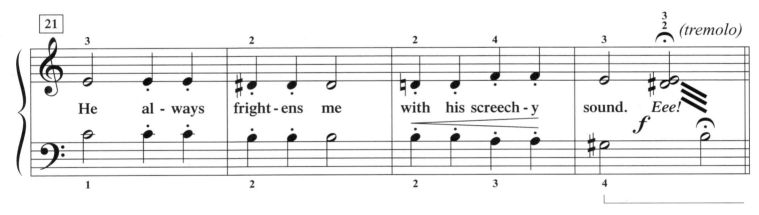

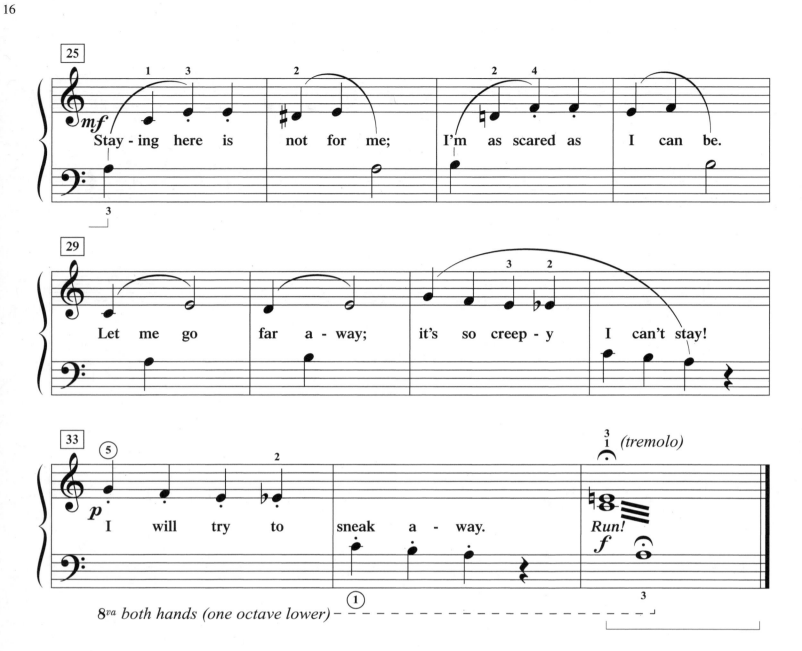

Halloween Comes Once a Year

Elizabeth W. Greenleaf

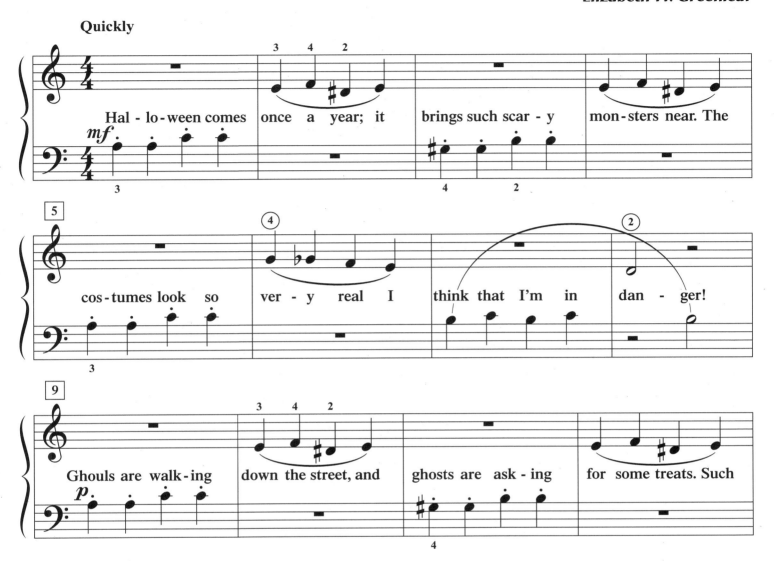

Teacher Duet: (Student plays 1 octave higher)

Copyright © 2003 The FJH Music Company Inc. (ASCAP).
International Copyright Secured.   Made in U.S.A.   All Rights Reserved.

FJH2153

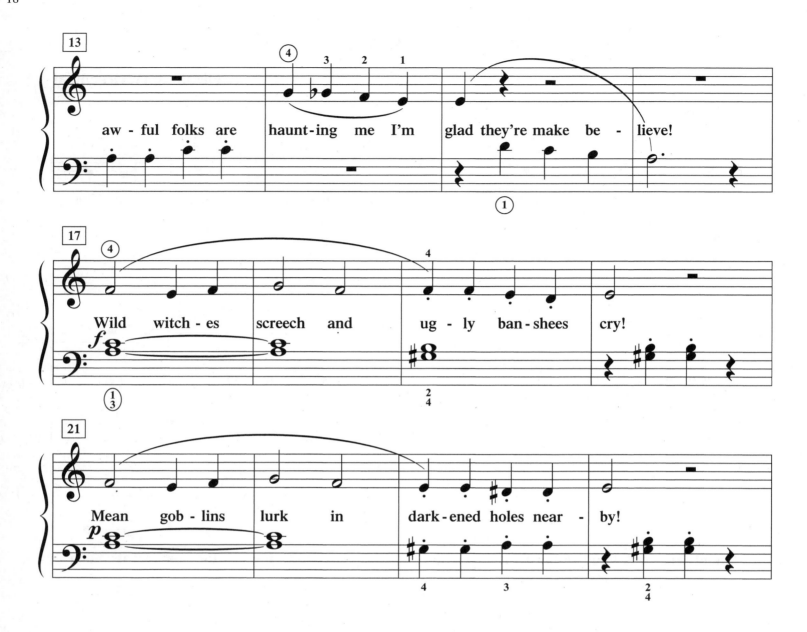

aw - ful folks are haunt-ing me I'm glad they're make be - lieve!

Wild witch - es screech and ug - ly ban - shees cry!

Mean gob - lins lurk in dark-ened holes near - by!

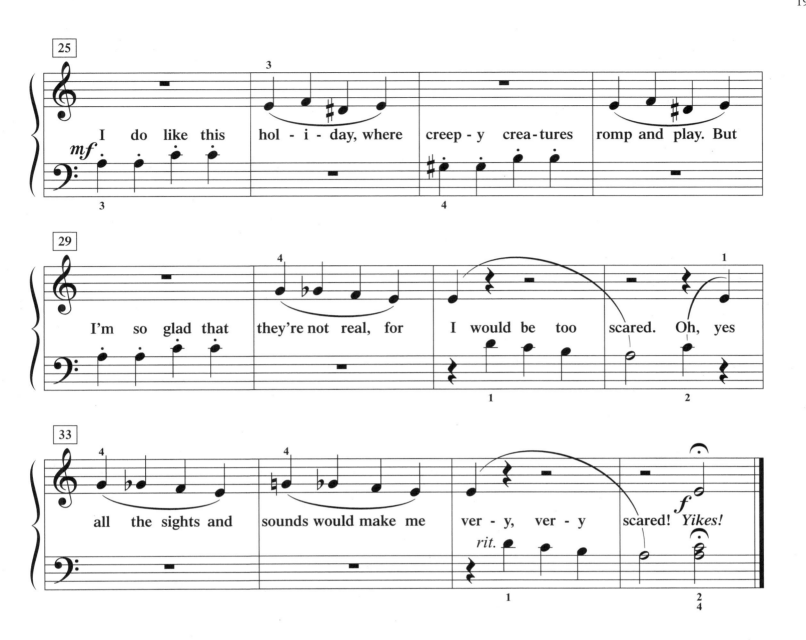

Greedy Goblins

Elizabeth W. Greenleaf

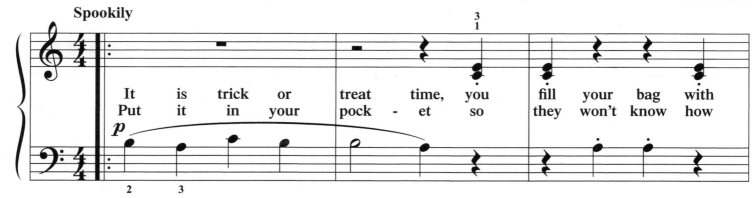

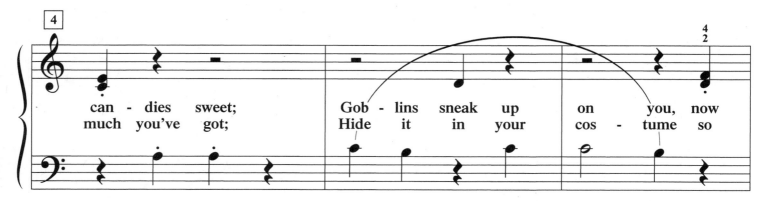

Teacher Duet: (Student plays 1 octave higher)

Copyright © 2002 The FJH Music Company Inc. (ASCAP).
International Copyright Secured.   Made in U.S.A.   All Rights Reserved.

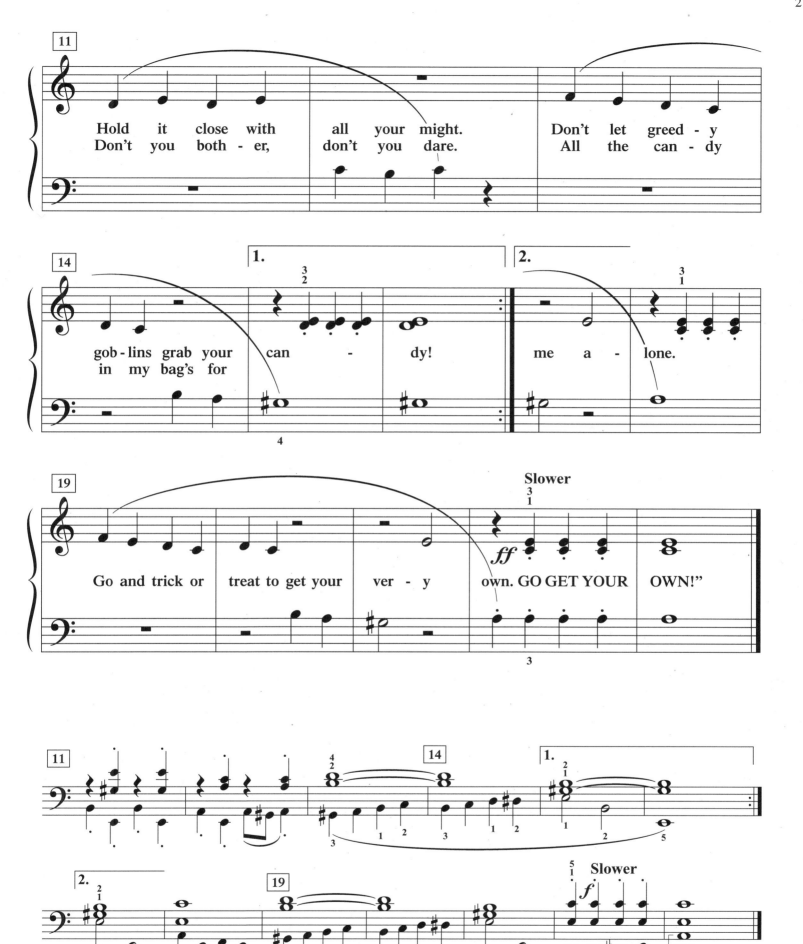

21

FJH2153

The Runaway Pumpkin

Elizabeth W. Greenleaf

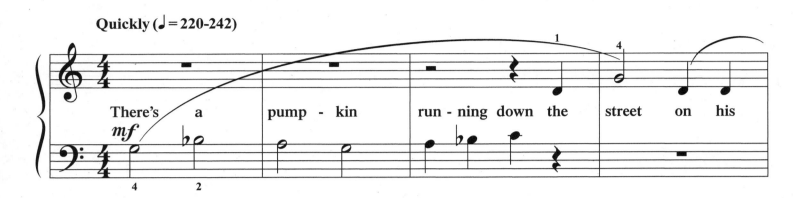

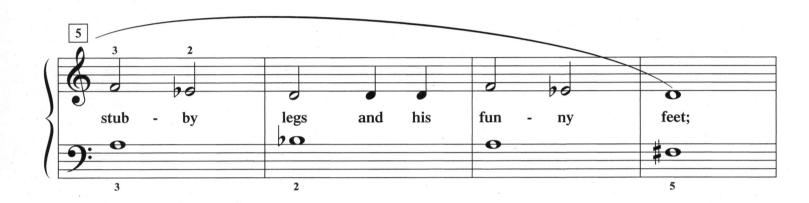

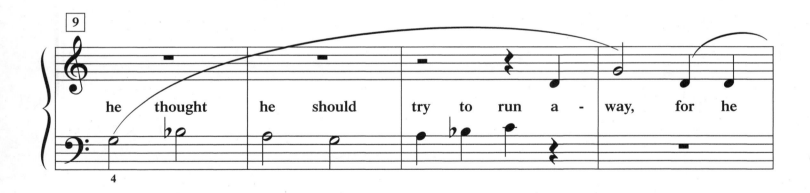

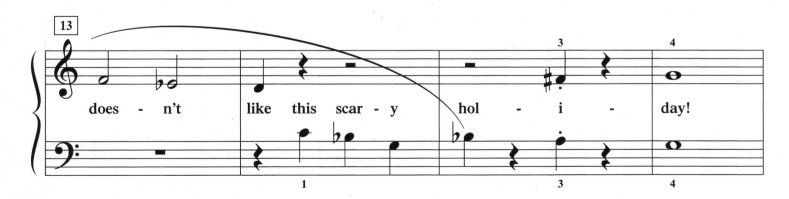

Copyright © 2005 The FJH Music Company Inc. (ASCAP).
International Copyright Secured.   Made in U.S.A.   All Rights Reserved.

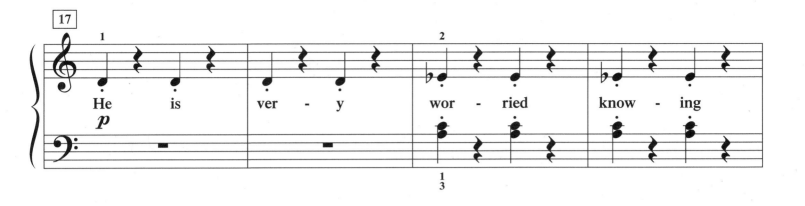

He is ver - y wor - ried know - ing

pump - kins get carved and then can - dles start glow - ing;

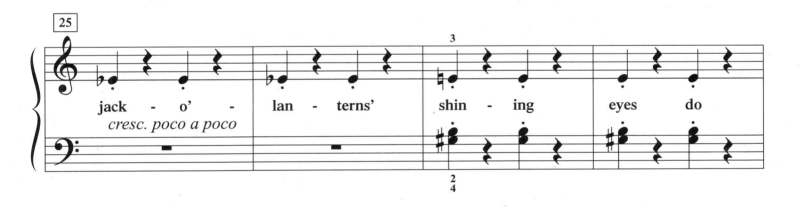

jack - o' - lan - terns' shin - ing eyes do

beck - on to chil - dren, "Come get a sur - prise!"

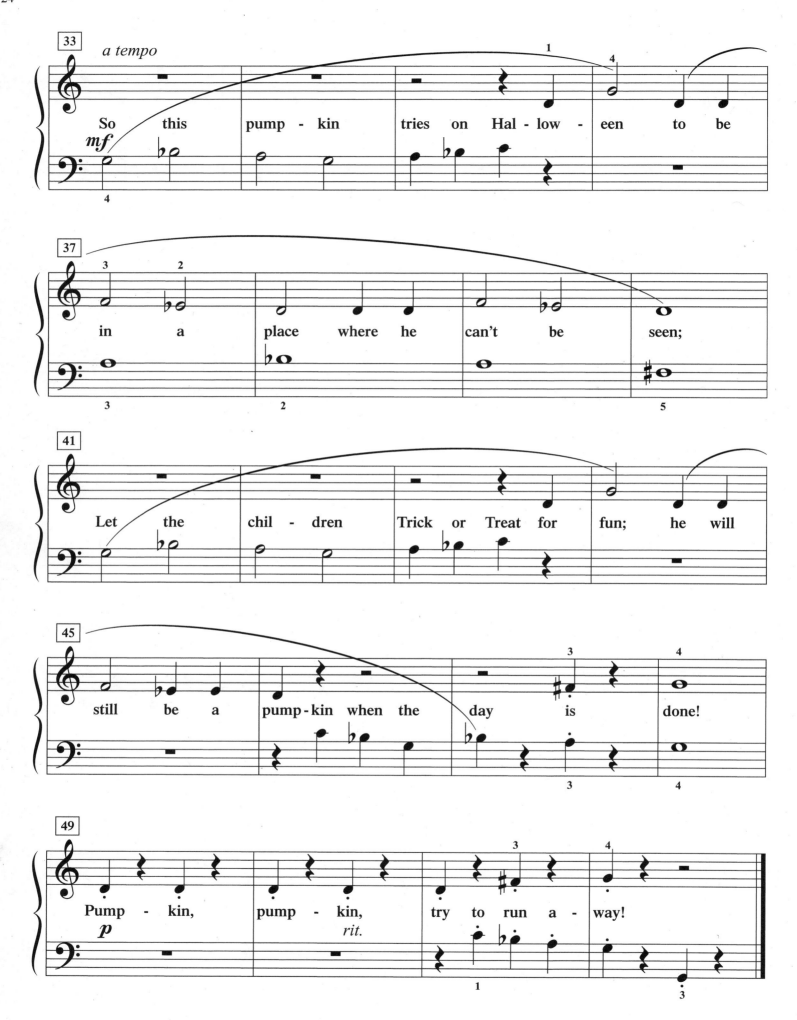